Listening to Leaders

# Why Should I Listen to FIREFIGHTERS?

Christine Honders

PowerKiDS press
NEW YORK

Published in 2020 by The Rosen Publishing Group, Inc.
29 East 21st Street, New York, NY 10010



Editor: Greg Roza
Book Design: Rachel Rising

Photo Credits: Cover (insert) © iStockphoto.com/FatCamera; Cover (background) Helen89/Shutterstock.com; p. 5 Sean Thomforde/Shutterstock.com; p. 7 Dan Holm/Shutterstock.com; p. 9 nikkytok/Shutterstock.com; p. 11 mon_ter/Shutterstock.com; p. 13 Africa Studio/Shutterstock.com; p. 15 Tsyb Oleh/Shutterstock.com; p. 17 evgenii mitroshin/Shutterstock.com; p. 19 Michael Blann/DigitalVision/Getty Images; p. 21 Jerry Sharp/Shutterstock.com; p. 22 Flashon Studio/Shutterstock.com.

Cataloging-in-Publication Data

Names: Honders, Christine.
Title: Why should I listen to firefighters? / Christine Honders.
Description: New York : PowerKids Press, 2020. | Series: Listening to leaders | Includes glossary and index.
Identifiers: LCCN ISBN 9781538341520 (pbk.) | ISBN 9781538341544 (library bound) | ISBN 9781538341537 (6 pack)
Subjects: LCSH: Fire fighters--Juvenile literature. | Fire prevention -- Juvenile literature.
Classification: LCC TH9148.H66 2019 | DDC 363.37--dc23

Manufactured in the United States of America

CPSIA Compliance Information: Batch #CSPK19 For further information contact Rosen Publishing, New York, New York at 1-800-237-9932.

# Contents

# The Dangers of Fire

Fires are scary and dangerous. It doesn't take much to start them. Once a fire starts it can spread very quickly. Fires destroy homes and seriously hurt people every year. That's why it's important for every family to learn about fire safety and **prevention**.

# Fire Safety Experts

Firefighters are **community** helpers trained to put out fires. They show up in minutes with water hoses and tools for rescuing people. Firefighters are also experts in fire safety. They go into schools and out into the community to teach people how to keep fires from starting in their homes.

28
MONHEIM
WARNING

# The First Step in Prevention

Firefighters recommend that every home has **smoke detectors**. Smoke detectors save lives every year. They should be placed high on the walls on each floor of the house, in the kitchen, and near bedrooms. Firefighters tell us to change smoke detector batteries every year to make sure they work properly.

## Too Hot in the Kitchen

Cooking is the number-one cause of house fires. Firefighters know how to prevent kitchen fires. Follow their advice. Never walk away from a boiling pot on the stove. Turn pot handles in so that no one will bump into them. Turn off appliances—such as stoves and ovens—when they are not in use.

# Stay Away from Matches!

Firefighters tell kids over and over never to play with matches. Matches are still the number-one cause of fire **injuries** and deaths for kids under five years old. Stay away from matches. You should also never play with lighters or lit candles.

# Hazards in the Home

Firefighters are brave and will run into burning buildings to help people. But it's up to us to help prevent home fires. Check your home for fire **hazards**. Never use broken electrical cords or chargers. Keep desk lamps away from curtains, blankets, and other fabrics.

# In Case of Fire

Firefighters recommend placing **fire extinguishers** in homes to put out small fires. But even with a small fire, call 9-1-1. If you're not sure what to do, leave and wait for the firefighters. Firefighters are the experts. They know the best way to put out fires caused by grease, electronics, or chemicals.

# What to Do in a House Fire

In case of a house fire, firefighters recommend dropping to the floor. Smoke rises, and it's easier to breathe near the ground. Use a piece of clothing to cover your mouth and nose. Then crawl to the nearest exit. Don't stop to take anything, and never, ever hide. If your clothing catches fire, stop, drop, and roll.

## Escape Plan

Families should have a fire escape plan. Firefighters say that everyone should know two ways out of every room in case an exit is blocked. Everyone should know where to meet outside. Families should practice their plans with fire drills. Never go back into a burning house! Let the firefighters do their jobs.

# Keeping Communities Safe

Over the past ten years, there have been fewer home fires. That's because firefighters in our communities work very hard to educate people about fire safety and prevention. The more we listen to our firefighters, the less likely we will ever experience a real fire.

# Glossary

**community:** The people living in an area and the area itself.

**fire extinguisher:** A container with chemicals that can be sprayed on a fire to put it out.

**hazard:** Something that could cause danger.

**injury:** Hurt or damage done to someone.

**prevention:** Keeping something from happening.

**smoke detector:** A device that can tell when a fire has started and lets people know with a loud noise.

# Index



# Websites

Due to the changing nature of Internet links, PowerKids Press has developed an online list of websites related to the subject of this book. This site is updated regularly. Please use this link to access the list: www.powerkidslinks.com/ltl/firefighters